Blessed
Are the
Peacemakers

Blessed Are the Peacemakers

Christ's Teachings about Love, Compassion & Forgiveness

Gathered & Introduced by Wendell Berry

Shoemaker $\substack{S \\ H}$ Hoard

"The Burden of the Gospels" first appeared in
The Christian Century

Library of Congress Cataloging-in-Publication Data
Bible. N.T. Gospels. English. Authorized. Selections. 2005.
Blessed are the peacemakers : Christ's teachings of love,
compassion, and forgiveness / gathered and introduced by
Wendell Berry.
p. cm.
ISBN (10) 1-59376-100-7
ISBN (13) 978-1-59376-100-4
1. Jesus Christ—Teachings. 2. Bible. N.T. Gospels
—Quotations. 3. Love—Religious aspects—Christianity—
Quotations, maxims, etc. 4. Peace—Religious aspects—
Christianity—Quotations, maxims, etc. I. Berry, Wendell,
1934- II. Title.

BS2415.A2 2005
226'.052036—DC22
2005023929

Book design by Gerilyn Attebery
Set in Sabon
Printed in the United States of America by Worzalla

Shoemaker Hoard
An Imprint of Avalon Publishing Group, Inc.
Distributed by Publishers Group West

10 9 8 7 6 5 4 3

Contents ❧

Introduction ∼

A NY OBSERVER WOULD HAVE TO say that Christianity is fashionable at present in the United States. This might be a good thing, except that the observer, observing more closely, would have to conclude that, to the extent that Christianity is fashionable, it is loosely fashionable. It seems to have remarkably little to do with the things that Jesus Christ actually taught.

Especially among Christians in positions of great wealth and power, the idea of reading the Gospels and keeping Jesus's commandments as stated therein has been replaced by a curious process of logic. According to this process, people first declare themselves to be followers of Christ, and then they assume that

3

whatever they say or do merits the adjective "Christian." (For don't we know that everybody named Rose smells like a rose?)

This process appears to have been dominant among Christian heads of state ever since Christianity became politically respectable. From this accommodation has proceeded a monstrous history of Christian violence. War after war has been prosecuted by bloodthirsty Christians, and to the profit of greedy Christians, as if Christ had never been born and the Gospels never written. I may have missed something, but I know of no Christian nation and no Christian leader from whose conduct the teachings of Christ could be inferred.

One cannot be aware both of the history of Christian war and of the contents of the Gospels without feeling that something is amiss. One may feel that, in the name of honesty, Christians ought either to quit fighting or quit calling themselves Christians. One way to see how far belligerent Christians have strayed from the words of Christ is to make a list, like the one presented in the following pages, of the Gospel passages in which Christ addresses explicitly the issues of human strife, forgiveness, compassion, and peacemaking.

The list that follows was made by me, with some help from friends. Other people's lists might differ somewhat, but I think they would be substantially the same. I have also included, in italics, the two passages that loose interpreters might interpret as justifying war: Matthew 10: 34–37 and Luke 22: 35–38. In both of these passages Christ is using the sword as a metaphor for the divisions He foresaw as results of His teaching and influence. If belligerent Christians wish to understand these passages literally, then they must explain why Christ speaks in the first passage only of "a" sword, and in the second of "two swords." He clearly was not raising an army. The many other passages gathered here deny the acceptability of the usual justifications for violence, official or otherwise.

The translation I have used is the King James Version, not only because of my love and respect for the language of that version, but also because it is the version that most English-speaking Christians have been reading for the last four hundred years while disobeying or ignoring Christ's commandments and praying for His help in their wars.

They have justified their disobedience on the grounds of the impracticality of obedience, though we have little proof of the practicality of disobedience, and precious few examples of obedience. The implication invariably has been that for a few feckless worshippers of God to obey Christ's commandments may be all right, but in practical matters such as war and preparation for war we will obey Caesar. The Christian followers of Caesar have thus committed themselves to an absurdity that they can neither resolve nor escape: the proposition that war can be made to serve peace; that you can make friends for love by hating and killing the enemies of love. This has never succeeded, and its failure is never acknowledged, which is a further absurdity.

The world's survival, so far, of this absurdity is explainable by the relative smallness, until recently, of the scale of war, and by the relative controllability, until now, of the most destructive weaponry. But now the scales of practicality have come to be differently weighted. The official terrorism of the Cold War and the doctrine of "mutual assured destruction" have already made us familiar with the ultimate absurdity: that we (or some other "we" equally devout and patriotic) may have to destroy the world in order to defend ourselves. To the surprise of some, no doubt, it is possible to look upon such an eventuality as impractical. To avoid it, we are going to need a better recourse than Caesar's. If we ever should become sane enough to reject total destruction as a means of victory, then, as my friend Wes Jackson once said to me, our evolutionary biologists will have to reckon how we could have received the best instruction for our survival two thousand years before it was most desperately needed.

Christ told us how to survive when He answered the question, Who is my neighbor? In the tenth chapter of Luke He tells the story of a Samaritan who cared for a Jew who had been badly wounded by thieves. As we know from the preceding chapter, in which the Disciples suggest in effect the firebombing of a Samaritan village, the Samaritans and the Jews were enemies. To modernize the story, then, and so to understand Christ's answer, we may substitute any other pair of enemies: fundamentalist Christian and fundamentalist Muslim, Palestinian and Israeli, captor and prisoner. The answer: Your neighbor is any sufferer who needs your help.

Matthew ⚬

CHAPTER 5

7   Blessed are the merciful: for they shall obtain mercy.

❧

9   Blessed are the peacemakers: for they shall be called the children of God.

❧

21   Ye have heard that it was said by them of old time, Thou shalt not kill; and whosoever shall kill shall be in danger of the judgment:

22   But I say unto you, That whosoever is angry with his brother without a cause shall be in danger of the judgment: and whosoever shall say to his brother, Raca, shall be in danger of the council: but whosoever shall say, Thou fool, shall be in danger of hell fire.

23 Therefore if thou bring thy gift to the altar, and there rememberest that thy brother hath ought against thee;

24 Leave there thy gift before the altar, and go thy way; first be reconciled to thy brother, and then come and offer thy gift.

25 Agree with thine adversary quickly, whiles thou art in the way with him; lest at any time the adversary deliver thee to the judge, and the judge deliver thee to the officer, and thou be cast into prison.

26 Verily I say unto thee, Thou shalt by no means come out thence, till thou hast paid the uttermost farthing.

❧

38 Ye have heard that it hath been said, An eye for an eye, and a tooth for a tooth:

39 But I say unto you, That ye resist not evil: but whosoever shall smite thee on thy right cheek, turn to him the other also.

40 And if any man will sue thee at the law, and take away thy coat, let him have thy cloke also.

41 And whosoever shall compel thee to go a mile, go with him twain.

42 Give to him that asketh thee, and from him that would borrow of thee turn not thou away.

❧

44 But I say unto you, Love your enemies, bless them that curse you, do good to them that hate you, and pray for them which despitefully use you, and persecute you;

45 That ye may be the children of your Father which is in heaven: for he maketh his sun to rise on the evil and on the good, and sendeth rain on the just and on the unjust.

CHAPTER 6

12   And forgive us our debts, as we
forgive our debtors.

&

14   For if ye forgive men their
trespasses, your heavenly Father
will also forgive you:

15   But if ye forgive not men their
trespasses, neither will your Father
forgive your trespasses.

CHAPTER 7

1   Judge not, that ye be not judged.

2   For with what judgment ye judge,
ye shall be judged: and with
what measure ye mete, it shall be
measured to you again.

3　And why beholdest thou the mote that is in thy brother's eye, but considerest not the beam that is in thine own eye?

4　Or how wilt thou say to thy brother, Let me pull out the mote out of thine eye; and, behold, a beam is in thine own eye?

5　Thou hypocrite, first cast out the beam out of thine own eye; and then shalt thou see clearly to cast out the mote out of thy brother's eye.

12　Therefore all things whatsoever ye would that men should do to you, do ye even so to them: for this is the law and the prophets.

CHAPTER 9

13   But go ye and learn what that
      meaneth, I will have mercy, and
      not sacrifice: for I am not come to
      call the righteous, but sinners to
      repentance.

CHAPTER 10

16   Behold, I send you forth as sheep in
      the midst of wolves: be ye therefore
      wise as serpents, and harmless as
      doves.

&

34   *Think not that I am come to send
      peace on earth: I came not to send
      peace, but a sword.*

35   *For I am come to set a man at*
variance against his father, and the
daughter against her mother, and
the daughter in law against her
mother in law.

36   *And a man's foes shall be they of his*
own household.

37   *He that loveth father or mother more*
than me is not worthy of me: and
he that loveth son or daughter more
than me is not worthy of me.

CHAPTER 12

7   But if ye had known what this
meaneth, I will have mercy, and
not sacrifice, ye would not have
condemned the guiltless.

14 Even so it is not the will of your Father which is in heaven, that one of these little ones should perish.

⸙

21 Then came Peter to him, and said, Lord, how oft shall my brother sin against me, and I forgive him? till seven times?

22 Jesus saith unto him, I say not unto thee, Until seven times: but, Until seventy times seven.

23 Therefore is the kingdom of heaven likened unto a certain king, which would take account of his servants.

24 And when he had begun to reckon, one was brought unto him, which owed him ten thousand talents.

25 But forasmuch as he had not to pay, his lord commanded him to be sold, and his wife, and children, and all that he had, and payment to be made.

26 The servant therefore fell down, and worshipped him, saying, Lord, have patience with me, and I will pay thee all.

27 Then the lord of that servant was moved with compassion, and loosed him, and forgave him the debt.

28 But the same servant went out, and found one of his fellowservants, which owed him an hundred pence: and he laid hands on him, and took him by the throat, saying, Pay me that thou owest.

29 And his fellowservant fell down at his feet, and besought him, saying, Have patience with me, and I will pay thee all.

30 And he would not: but went and cast him into prison, till he should pay the debt.

31 So when his fellowservants saw what was done, they were very sorry, and came and told unto their lord all that was done.

32 Then his lord, after that he had
called him, said unto him, O thou
wicked servant, I forgave thee all
that debt, because thou desiredst me:

33 Shouldest not thou also have had
compassion on thy fellowservant,
even as I had pity on thee?

34 And his lord was wroth, and
delivered him to the tormentors, till
he should pay all that was due unto
him.

35 So likewise shall my heavenly
Father do also unto you, if ye from
your hearts forgive not every one
his brother their trespasses.

CHAPTER 25

34 Then shall the King say unto
them on his right hand, Come, ye
blessed of my Father, inherit the
kingdom prepared for you from the
foundation of the world:

35 For I was an hungred, and ye gave me meat: I was thirsty, and ye gave me drink: I was a stranger, and ye took me in:

36 Naked, and ye clothed me: I was sick, and ye visited me: I was in prison, and ye came unto me.

37 Then shall the righteous answer him, saying, Lord, when saw we thee an hungred, and fed thee? or thirsty, and gave thee drink?

38 When saw we thee a stranger, and took thee in? or naked, and clothed thee?

39 Or when saw we thee sick, or in prison, and came unto thee?

40 And the King shall answer and say unto them, Verily I say unto you, Inasmuch as ye have done it unto one of the least of these my brethren, ye have done it unto me.

CHAPTER 26

50 And Jesus said unto him [Judas], Friend, wherefore art thou come? Then came they, and laid hands on Jesus, and took him.

51 And, behold, one of them which were with Jesus stretched out his hand, and drew his sword, and struck a servant of the high priest's, and smote off his ear.

52 Then said Jesus unto him, Put up again thy sword into his place: for all they that take the sword shall perish with the sword.

Mark ❧

25   And when ye stand praying,
     forgive, if ye have ought against
     any: that your Father also which
     is in heaven may forgive you your
     trespasses.

26   But if ye do not forgive, neither
     will your Father which is in heaven
     forgive your trespasses.

Luke ❧

76 And thou, child, shalt be called the prophet of the Highest: for thou shalt go before the face of the Lord to prepare his ways;

77 To give knowledge of salvation unto his people by the remission of their sins,

78 Through the tender mercy of our God; whereby the dayspring from on high hath visited us,

79 To give light to them that sit in darkness and in the shadow of death, to guide our feet into the way of peace.*

---

*This passage is spoken by Zacharias to his infant son who would be known as John the Baptist.

CHAPTER 2

13 And suddenly there was with the angel a multitude of the heavenly host praising God, and saying,

14 Glory to God in the highest, and on earth peace, good will toward men.

CHAPTER 3

14 And the soldiers likewise demanded of him [John the Baptist], saying, And what shall we do? And he said unto them, Do violence to no man, neither accuse any falsely; and be content with your wages.

CHAPTER 6

27 But I say unto you which hear, Love your enemies, do good to them which hate you,

28 Bless them that curse you, and pray for them which despitefully use you.

29 And unto him that smiteth thee on the one cheek offer also the other; and him that taketh away thy cloke forbid not to take thy coat also.

30 Give to every man that asketh of thee; and of him that taketh away thy goods ask them not again.

31 And as ye would that men should do to you, do ye also to them likewise.

32 For if ye love them which love you, what thank have ye? for sinners also love those that love them.

33 And if ye do good to them which do good to you, what thank have ye? for sinners also do even the same.

34 And if ye lend to them of whom ye hope to receive, what thank have ye? for sinners also lend to sinners, to receive as much again.

35   But love ye your enemies, and do good, and lend, hoping for nothing again; and your reward shall be great, and ye shall be the children of the Highest: for he is kind unto the unthankful and to the evil.

36   Be ye therefore merciful, as your Father also is merciful.

37   Judge not, and ye shall not be judged: condemn not, and ye shall not be condemned: forgive, and ye shall be forgiven:

38   Give, and it shall be given unto you; good measure, pressed down, and shaken together, and running over, shall men give into your bosom. For with the same measure that ye mete withal it shall be measured to you again.

◈

46   And why call ye me, Lord, Lord, and do not the things which I say?

CHAPTER 9

52   And [Jesus] sent messengers before his face: and they went, and entered into a village of the Samaritans, to make ready for him.

53   And they did not receive him, because his face was as though he would go to Jerusalem.*

54   And when his disciples James and John saw this, they said, Lord, wilt thou that we command fire to come down from heaven, and consume them, even as Elias did?

55   But he turned, and rebuked them, and said, Ye know not what manner of spirit ye are of.

56   For the Son of man is not come to destroy men's lives, but to save them. And they went to another village.

---

*That is, He was a Jew, whom the Samaritans regarded as an enemy.

CHAPTER 10

25   And, behold, a certain lawyer
     stood up, and tempted him, saying,
     Master, what shall I do to inherit
     eternal life?

26   He said unto him, What is written
     in the law? how readest thou?

27   And he answering said, Thou shalt
     love the Lord thy God with all thy
     heart, and with all thy soul, and
     with all thy strength, and with all
     thy mind; and thy neighbour as
     thyself.

28   And he said unto him, Thou hast
     answered right: this do, and thou
     shalt live.

29   But he, willing to justify himself,
     said unto Jesus, And who is my
     neighbour?

30 And Jesus answering said, A certain man went down from Jerusalem to Jericho, and fell among thieves, which stripped him of his raiment, and wounded him, and departed, leaving him half dead.

31 And by chance there came down a certain priest that way: and when he saw him, he passed by on the other side.

32 And likewise a Levite, when he was at the place, came and looked on him, and passed by on the other side.

33 But a certain Samaritan, as he journeyed, came where he was: and when he saw him, he had compassion on him,

34 And went to him, and bound up his wounds, pouring in oil and wine, and set him on his own beast, and brought him to an inn, and took care of him.

35 And on the morrow when he departed, he took out two pence, and gave them to the host, and said unto him, Take care of him; and whatsoever thou spendest more, when I come again, I will repay thee.

36 Which now of these three, thinkest thou, was neighbour unto him that fell among the thieves?

37 And he said, He that shewed mercy on him. Then said Jesus unto him, Go, and do thou likewise.

CHAPTER 17

3 Take heed to yourselves: If thy brother trespass against thee, rebuke him; and if he repent, forgive him.

4 And if he trespass against thee seven times in a day, and seven times in a day turn again to thee, saying, I repent; thou shalt forgive him.

CHAPTER 22

24 And there was also a strife among them, which of them should be accounted the greatest.

25 And he said unto them, The kings of the Gentiles exercise lordship over them; and they that exercise authority upon them are called benefactors.

26 But ye shall not be so: but he that is greatest among you, let him be as the younger; and he that is chief, as he that doth serve.

27 For whether is greater, he that sitteth at meat, or he that serveth? is not he that sitteth at meat? but I am among you as he that serveth.

❧

35 *And he said unto them, When I sent you without purse, and scrip, and shoes, lacked ye any thing? And they said, Nothing.*

36   *Then said he unto them, But now, he that hath a purse, let him take it, and likewise his scrip: and he that hath no sword, let him sell his garment, and buy one.*

37   *For I say unto you, that this that is written must yet be accomplished in me, And he was reckoned among the transgressors: for the things concerning me have an end.*

38   *And they said, Lord, behold, here are two swords. And he said unto them, It is enough.*

❧

49   When they which were about him saw what would follow, they said unto him, Lord, shall we smite with the sword?

50   And one of them smote the servant of the high priest, and cut off his right ear.

51   And Jesus answered and said, Suffer ye thus far. And he touched his ear, and healed him.

33   And when they were come to the place, which is called Calvary, there they crucified him, and the malefactors, one on the right hand, and the other on the left.

34   Then said Jesus, Father, forgive them; for they know not what they do. And they parted his raiment, and cast lots.

John ❧

4   They say unto him, Master, this woman was taken in adultery, in the very act.

5   Now Moses in the law commanded us, that such should be stoned: but what sayest thou?

6   This they said, tempting him, that they might have to accuse him. But Jesus stooped down, and with his finger wrote on the ground, as though he heard them not.

7   So when they continued asking him, he lifted up himself, and said unto them, He that is without sin among you, let him first cast a stone at her.

8   And again he stooped down, and wrote on the ground.

9   And they which heard it, being convicted by their own conscience, went out one by one, beginning at the eldest, even unto the last: and Jesus was left alone, and the woman standing in the midst.

10   When Jesus had lifted up himself, and saw none but the woman, he said unto her, Woman, where are those thine accusers? hath no man condemned thee?

11   She said, No man, Lord. And Jesus said unto her, Neither do I condemn thee: go, and sin no more.

CHAPTER 14

15   If ye love me, keep my commandments.

CHAPTER 18

10   Then Simon Peter having a sword
     drew it, and smote the high priest's
     servant, and cut off his right ear.
     The servant's name was Malchus.

11   Then said Jesus unto Peter, Put up
     thy sword into the sheath: the cup
     which my Father hath given me,
     shall I not drink it?

The Burden of the Gospels

ANYBODY HALF AWAKE THESE DAYS WILL be aware that there are many Christians who are exceedingly confident in their understanding of the Gospels, and who are exceedingly self-confident in their understanding of themselves in their faith. They appear to know precisely the purposes of God, and they appear to be perfectly assured that they are now doing, and in every circumstance will continue to do, precisely God's will as it applies specifically to themselves. They are confident, moreover, that God hates people whose faith differs from their own, and they are happy to concur in that hatred.

Having been invited to speak to a convocation of Christian seminarians, I at first felt

that I should say nothing until I confessed that
I do not have any such confidence. And then
I understood that this would have to be my
subject. I would have to speak of the meaning,
as I understand it, of my lack of confidence,
which I think is not at all the same as a lack
of faith.

It is a fact that I have spent my life, for
the most part willingly, under the influence
of the Bible, particularly the Gospels, and of
the Christian tradition in literature and the
other arts. As a child, sometimes unwilling-
ly, I learned many of the Bible's stories and
teachings, and was affected more than I knew
by the language of the King James Version,
which is the translation I still prefer. For most
of my adult life I have been an urgently in-
terested and frequently uneasy reader of the
Bible, particularly of the Gospels. At the
same time I have tried to be a worthy reader
of Dante, Milton, Herbert, Blake, Eliot, and
other poets of the Christian tradition. As a
result of this reading and of my experience, I
am by principle and often spontaneously, as
if by nature, a man of faith. But my reading
of the Gospels, comforting and clarifying and
instructive as they frequently are, deeply mov-
ing or exhilarating as they frequently are, has

caused me to understand them also as a burden, sometimes raising the hardest of personal questions, sometimes bewildering, sometimes contradictory, sometimes apparently outrageous in their demands. This is the confession of an unconfident reader.

∾

I will begin by dealing with the embarrassing questions that the Gospels impose, I imagine, upon any serious reader. There are two of these, and the first is this: If you had been living in Jesus's time and had heard Him teaching, would you have been one of His followers? To be an honest taker of this test, I think you have to try to forget that you have read the Gospels and that Jesus has been a "big name" for two thousand years. You have to imagine instead that you are walking past the local courthouse and you come upon a crowd listening to a man named Joe Green or Green Joe, depending on judgments whispered among the listeners on the fringe. You too stop to listen, and you soon realize that Joe Green is saying something utterly scandalous, utterly unexpectable from the premises of modern society. He is saying: "Don't resist evil. If somebody slaps your right cheek, let him slap your left cheek too. Love your enemies. When people curse you, you must bless them. When people hate you, you must treat them kindly. When people mistrust you, you must pray for them. This is the way you must act if you want to be children of God." Well, you know how happily *that* would be received, not only in the White House and the Capitol, but among most of your neighbors. And then suppose this Joe Green looks at you over the heads of the crowd, calls you by name, and says, "I want to come to dinner at your house."

I suppose that you, like me, hope very much that you would say, "Come ahead." But I suppose also that you, like me, had better not be too sure. You will remember that in Jesus's lifetime even His most intimate friends could hardly be described as overconfident.

The second question is this—it comes right after the verse in which Jesus says, "If you love me, keep my commandments." Can you be sure that you would keep His commandments if it became excruciatingly painful to do so? And here I need to tell another story, this time one that actually happened.

In 1569, in Holland, a Mennonite named Dirk Willems, under threat of capital sentence as a heretic, was fleeing from arrest, pursued by a "thief catcher." As they ran across a frozen body of water, the thief-catcher broke through the ice. Without help, he would have drowned. What did Dirk Willems do then?

Was the thief-catcher an enemy merely to be hated, or was he a neighbor to be loved as one loves oneself? Was he an enemy whom one must love in order to be a child of God? Was he "one of the least of these my brethren"?

What Dirk Willems did was turn back, put out his hands to his pursuer, and save his life. The thief-catcher, who then of course wanted to let his rescuer go, was forced to arrest him. Dirk Willems was brought to trial, sentenced, and burned to death by a "lingering fire."

I, and I suppose you, would like to be a child of God even at the cost of so much pain. But would we, in similar circumstances, turn back to offer the charity of Christ to an enemy? Again, I don't think we ought to be too sure. We should remember that "Christian" generals and heads of state have routinely thanked God for the deaths of their enemies, and that the persecutors of 1569 undoubtedly thanked God for the capture and death of the "heretic" Dirk Willems.

Those are peculiar questions. I don't think we can escape them, if we are honest. And if we are honest, I don't think we can answer them. We humans, as we well know, have repeatedly been surprised by what we will or won't do under pressure. A person may come to be, as many have been, heroically faithful in great adversity, but as long as that person is alive we can only say that he or she did well but remains under the requirement to *do* well. As long as we are alive, there is always a next time, and so the questions remain. These are questions we must live with, regarding them as unanswerable and yet profoundly influential.

⟊

The other burdening problems of the Gospels that I want to talk about are like those questions in that they are not solvable but can only be lived with as a sort of continuing education. These problems, however, are not so personal or dramatic but are merely issues of reading and making sense.

As a reader, I am unavoidably a writer. Many years of trying to write what I have perceived to be true have taught me that there are limits to what a human mind can know, and limits to what a human language can say. One may believe, as I do, in inspiration, but one must believe knowing that even the most inspired are limited in what they can tell of what they know. We humans write and read, teach and learn, at the inevitable cost of falling short. The language that reveals also obscures. And these qualifications that bear on any writing must bear of course on the Gospels.

I need to say also that, as a reader, I am first of all a literalist, as I think every reader should be. This does not mean that I don't appreciate Jesus's occasional irony or sarcasm ("They have their reward"), or that I am against interpretation, or that I don't believe in "higher levels of meaning." It certainly does not mean that I think every word of the Bible is equally true, or that "literalist" is a synonym for "fundamentalist." I mean simply that I expect any writing to make literal sense before making sense of any other kind. Interpretation should not contradict or otherwise violate the literal meaning. To read the Gospels as a literalist is, to me, the way to take them as seriously as possible.

But to take the Gospels seriously, to assume that they say what they mean and mean what they say, is the beginning of troubles. Those would-be literalists who yet argue that the Bible is unerring and unquestionable have not dealt with its contradictions, which of course it does contain, and the Gospels are not exempt. Some of Jesus's instructions are burdensome, not because they involve contradiction, but merely because they are so demanding. The proposition that love, forgiveness, and peaceableness are the only neighborly relationships that are acceptable to God is difficult for us weak and violent humans, but it is plain enough for any literalist. We must either accept it as an absolute or absolutely reject it. The same for the proposition that we are not permitted to choose our neighbors ahead of time or to limit neighborhood, as is plain from the parable of the Samaritan. The same for the requirement that we must be perfect, like God, which seems as outrageous as the Buddhist vow to "save all sentient beings," and perhaps is meant to measure and instruct us in the same way. It is, to say the least, unambiguous.

But what, for example, are we to make of Luke 14:26: "If any man come to me, and hate not his father, and mother, and wife, and children, and brethren, and sisters, yea, and his own life also, he cannot be my disciple."

This contradicts not only the fifth command-
ment but Jesus's own instruction to "Love thy
neighbor as thyself." It contradicts His obedience to his mother at the marriage in Cana of
Galilee. It contradicts the concern He shows
for the relatives of his friends and followers.
But the word in the King James Version is
"hate." If you go to the New English Bible or
the New Revised Standard Version, looking
for relief, the word still is "hate." This clearly
is the sort of thing that leads to "biblical ex-
egesis." My own temptation is to become a lit-
erary critic, wag my head learnedly, and say,
"Well, this obviously is a bit of hyperbole—
the sort of exaggeration a teacher would use
to shock his students awake." Maybe so, but
it is not obviously so, and it comes perilously
close to "He didn't really mean it"—always
a risky assumption when reading, and especially dangerous when reading the Gospels.
Another possibility, and I think a better one,
is to accept our failure to understand, not as
a misstatement or a textual flaw or as a prob-
lem to be solved, but as a question to live with
and a burden to be borne.

We may say with some reason that such
apparent difficulties might be resolved if we
knew more, a further difficulty being that

we *don't* know more. The Gospels, like all other written works, impose on their readers the burden of their incompleteness. However partial we may be to the doctrine of the true account or "realism," we must concede at last that reality is inconceivably great and any representation of it necessarily incomplete.

St. John at the end of his Gospel, remembering perhaps the third verse of his first chapter, makes a charming acknowledgement of this necessary incompleteness: "And there are also many other things which Jesus did, the which, if they should be written every one, I suppose that even the world itself could not contain the books that should be written." Our darkness, then, is not going to be completely lighted. Our ignorance finally is irremediable. We humans are never going to know everything, even assuming we have the capacity, because for reasons of the most insistent practicality we can't be told everything. We need to remember here Jesus's repeated admonitions to his disciples: You don't know; you don't understand; you've got it wrong.

The Gospels, then, stand at the opening of a mystery in which our lives are deeply, dangerously, and inescapably involved. This is a mystery that the Gospels can only partially reveal, for it could be fully revealed only by more books than the world could contain. It is a mystery that we are condemned but also are highly privileged to live our way into, trusting properly that to our little knowledge greater knowledge may be revealed. It is this privilege that should make us wary of any attempt to reduce faith to a rigmarole of judgments and explanations, or to any sort of familiar talk about God. Reductive religion is just as objectionable as reductive science, and for the same reason: Reality is large, and our minds are small.

❧

And so the issue of reality—What is the *scope* of reality? What is real?—emerges as the crisis of this discussion. Right at the heart of the religious impulse there seems to be a certain solicitude for reality: the fear of foreclosing it or of reducing it to some merely human estimate. Many of us are still refusing to trust Caesar, in any of his modern incarnations, with the power to define reality. Many of us are still refusing to entrust that power to science. As inhabitants of the modern world, we are religious now perhaps to the extent of our desire to crack open the coffin of materialism, and to give to reality a larger, freer definition than is allowed by the militant materialists of the corporate economy and their political servants, or by the mechanical paradigm of reductive science. Or perhaps I can make most plain what I'm trying to get at if I say that many of us are still withholding credence, just as properly and for the same reasons, from any person or institution claiming to have the definitive word on the purposes and the mind of God.

It seems to me that all the religions I know anything about emerge from an instinct to push against any merely human constraints on reality. In the Bible such constraints are conventionally attributed to "the world" in the pejorative sense of that term, which we may define as the world of the creation *reduced* by any of the purposes of selfishness. The contrary purpose, the purpose of freedom, is stated by Jesus in the fourth Gospel: "I am come that they might have life, and that they might have it more abundantly."

This astonishing statement can be thought about and understood endlessly, for it is endlessly meaningful, but I don't think it calls for much in the way of interpretation. It does call for a very strict and careful reading of the word "life."

To talk about or to desire more abundance of anything has probably always been dangerous, but it seems particularly dangerous now. In an age of materialist science, economics, art, and politics, we ought not to be much shocked by the appearance of materialist religion. We know we don't have to look far to find people who equate more abundant life with a bigger car, a bigger house, a bigger bank account, and a bigger church. They are wrong, of course. If Jesus meant only that we should have more possessions or even more "life expectancy," then John 10:10 is no more remarkable than an advertisement for any commodity whatever. Abundance, in this verse, cannot refer to an abundance of material possessions, for life does not require a material abundance; it requires only a material sufficiency. That sufficiency granted, life itself, which is a membership in the living world, is already an abundance.

But even life in this generous sense of membership in creation does not protect us, as we know, from the dangers of avarice, of selfishness, of the wrong kind of abundance. Those dangers can be overcome only by the realization that in speaking of more abundant life, Jesus is not proposing to free *us* by making us richer; he is proposing to set *life* free from precisely that sort of error. He is talking about life, which is only incidentally our life, as a limitless reality.

∽

Now that I have come out against materialism, I fear that I will be expected to say something in favor of spirituality. But if I am going to go on in the direction of what Jesus meant by "life" and "more abundantly," then I have got to avoid that duality of matter and spirit at all costs.

As every reader knows, the Gospels are overwhelmingly concerned with the conduct of human life, of life in the human commonwealth. In the Sermon on the Mount and in other places Jesus is asking his followers to see that the way to more abundant life is the way of love. We are to love one another, and this love is to be more comprehensive than our love for family and friends and tribe and nation. We are to love our neighbors though they may be strangers to us. We are to love our enemies. And this is to be a practical love; it is to be practiced, here and now. Love evidently is not just a feeling but is indistinguishable from the willingness to help, to be useful to one another. The way of love is indistinguishable, moreover, from the way of freedom. We don't need much imagination to imagine that to be free of hatred, of enmity, of the endless and hopeless effort to oppose violence with violence, would be to have life more abundantly. To be free of indifference would be to have life more abundantly. To be free of the insane rationalizations for our desire to kill one another—that surely would be to have life more abundantly.

And where more than in the Gospels' teaching about love do we see that famously estranged pair, matter and spirit, melt and flow together? There was a Samaritan who came upon one of his enemies, a Jew, lying wounded beside the road. And the Samaritan had compassion on the Jew and bound up his wounds and took care of him. Was this help spiritual or material? Was the Samaritan's compassion earthly or heavenly? If those questions confuse us, that is only because we have for so long allowed ourselves to believe, as if to divide reality impartially between science and religion, that material life and spiritual life, earthly life and heavenly life, are two different things.

To get unconfused, let us go to a further and even more interesting question about the parable of the Samaritan: Why? Why did the Samaritan reach out in love to his enemy, a Jew, who happened also to be his neighbor? Why was the unbounding of this love so important to Jesus?

We might reasonably answer, remembering Genesis 1:27, that all humans, friends and enemies alike, have the same dignity, deserve the same respect, and are worthy of the same compassion because they are, all alike, made in God's image. That is enough of a mystery, and it implies enough obligation, to waylay us a while. It is certainly something we need to bear anxiously in mind. But it is also too human-centered, too potentially egotistical, to leave alone.

I think Jesus recommended the Samaritan's loving-kindness, what certain older writers called "holy living," simply as a matter of propriety, for the Samaritan was living in what Jesus understood to be a holy world. The foreground of the Gospels is occupied by human beings and the issues of their connection to one another and to God. But there is a background, and the background more often than not is the world in the best sense of the word, the world as made, approved, loved, sustained, and finally to be redeemed by God. Much of the action and the talk of the Gospels takes place outdoors: on mountainsides, lake shores, river banks, in fields and pastures, places populated not only by humans but by animals and plants, both domestic and wild. And these non-human creatures, sheep and lilies and birds, are always represented as worthy of, or as flourishing within, the love and the care of God.

To know what to make of this, we need to look back to the Old Testament, to Genesis, to the Psalms, to the preoccupation with the relation of the Israelites to their land that runs through the whole lineage of the prophets. Through all this, much is implied or taken for granted. In only two places that I remember is the always implicit relation—the practical or working relation—of God to the creation plainly stated. Psalm 104:30, addressing God and speaking of the creatures, says, "Thou sendest forth thy spirit, they are created..." And, as if in response, Elihu says to Job (34:14–15) that if God "gather unto himself his spirit and his breath; All flesh shall perish together..." I have cut Elihu's sentence a little short so as to leave the emphasis on the phrase "all flesh."

Those also are verses that don't require interpretation, but I want to stretch them out in paraphrase just to make as plain as possible my reason for quoting them. They are saying that not just humans but *all* creatures live by participating in the life of God, by partaking of His spirit and breathing His breath.* And so the Samaritan reaches out in love to help his enemy, breaking all the customary boundaries, because he has clearly seen in his enemy not only a neighbor, not only a fellow human or a fellow creature, but a fellow sharer in the life of God.

When Jesus speaks of having life more abundantly, this, I think, is the life He means: a life that is not reducible by division, category, or degree, but is one thing, heavenly and earthly, spiritual and material, divided only insofar as it is embodied in distinct creatures. He is talking about a finite world that is infinitely holy, a world of time that is filled with life that is eternal. His offer of more abundant life, then,

---

*We now know that this relationship is even more complex, more utterly inclusive and whole, than the biblical writers suspected. Some scientists would insist that the conventional priority given to living creatures over the nonliving is misleading. Try, for example to separate life from the lifeless minerals on which life depends.

is not an invitation to declare ourselves as certified "Christians," but rather to become conscious, consenting, and responsible participants in the one great life, a fulfillment hardly institutional at all.

To be convinced of the sanctity of the world, and to be mindful of a human vocation to responsible membership in such a world, must always have been a burden. But it is a burden that falls with greatest weight on us humans of the industrial age who have been and are, by any measure, the humans most guilty of desecrating the world and of destroying creation. And we ought to be a little terrified to realize that, for the most part and at least for the time being, we are helplessly guilty. It seems as though industrial humanity has brought about phase two of original sin. We all are now complicit in the murder of creation. We certainly do know how to apply better measures to our conduct and our work. We know how to do far better than we are doing. But we don't know how to extricate ourselves from our complicity very surely or very soon. How could we live without degrading our soils, slaughtering our forests, polluting our streams, poisoning the air and the rain? How could we live without the ozone hole and the hypoxic zones? How could we live without endangering species, including our own? How could we live without the war economy and the holocaust of the fossil fuels? To the offer of more abundant life, we have chosen to respond with the economics of extinction.

If we take the Gospels seriously, we are left, in our dire predicament, facing an utterly humbling question: How must we live and work so as not to be estranged from God's presence in His work and in all His creatures? The answer, we may say, is given in Jesus's teaching about love. But that answer raises another question that plunges us into the abyss of our ignorance, which is both human and peculiarly modern: How are we to make of that love an economic practice?

That question calls for many answers, and we don't know most of them. It is a question that those humans who want to answer will be living and working with for a long time—if they are allowed a long time. Meanwhile, may Heaven guard us from those who think they already have the answers.

Author of more than forty books of fiction, poetry, and essays, WENDELL BERRY has farmed a hillside in his native Henry County, Kentucky, for forty years. He has received numerous awards for his work, including the T. S. Eliot Award, the Aiken Taylor Award for poetry, and the John Hay Award of the Orion Society.